PLANNING MY OWN FUNERAL?

Stephen Joseph Wolf

idjc press

Planning My Own Funeral?
Copyright © 2009
Stephen Joseph Wolf

All rights reserved. No part of this book may be copied or reproduced in any form or by any means, except for the planning worksheets by the owner of this book for his or her personal use or the inclusion of brief quotations in a review, without the written permission of the author or publisher.

Scripture texts used in this work are taken from the *New American Bible,* copyright © 1991, 1986, and 1970 by the Confraternity of Christian Doctrine, Washington, DC 20017 and are used by permission of the copyright owner. All rights reserved.

Prayer from the Prefaces is drawn from the English translation of *The Roman Missal* Copyright © 1973, International Committee on English in the Liturgy, ICEL. All rights reserved.

A Testament of Life (pgs. 13-16) is from Anthony de Mello, S.J., *Wellsprings: A Book of Spiritual Exercises* © Copyright 1986, Doubleday, and *Hearts on Fire: Praying with Jesuits,* edited by Michael Harter, S.J., Institute of Jesuit Sources, 1993. All rights reserved.

The readings captions (pg. 27-32), description of symbols (pg. 41-43), and litany (pg. 66) are drawn from the *Order of Christian Funerals,* Copyright © 1989, 1985, ICEL. All rights reserved.

Closing prayer (pg. 36) and *Blessing of a Son or Daughter* (pg. 64) are from the English translation of the *Book of Blessings* Copyright © 1987, ICEL. All rights reserved.

Thanks be to Ronald Rolheiser for the reflections on the blessing of an elder from *Against An Infinite Horizon,* Copyright © 2001, New York: Random House, Inc. All rights reserved.

Planning My own Funeral? was originally compiled for the *FIAT (Faith In Action Together) Groups* of St. Stephen Catholic Community in Hermitage, Old Hickory, & Mt. Juliet, Tennessee.

Thanks to Cecilia Thomas, for use of the cover art by the author.

Printed in the U.S.A. and distributed by Ingram Books

ISBN 978-0-9795549-6-4

Additional copies are available from
St. Mary's Bookstore in Nashville, Tennessee
www.stmarysbookstore.com,
www.amazon.com, and other fine bookstores.

PRAYER FROM THE PREFACES

Father, all-powerful and ever-living God,
we do well always and everywhere to give you thanks
through Jesus Christ our Lord.
In him, who rose from the dead,
our hope of resurrection dawned.
The sadness of death gives way
to the bright promise of [eternal life].
Lord, for your faithful people life is changed, not ended.
When the body of our earthly dwelling lies in death
we gain an everlasting dwelling place in heaven...
...[Our Lord Jesus Christ] gave his life
that we might live to you alone for ever...
...In him the world is saved, [humanity] is reborn,
and the dead rise again to life...
...By your power you bring us to birth.
By your providence you rule our lives.
By your command you free us at last from sin
as we return to the dust from which we came.
Through the saving death of your Son
we rise at your word to the glory of the resurrection...
...Death is the just reward for our sins,
yet, when at last we die,
your loving kindness calls us back to life
in company with Christ, whose victory is redemption.
Our hearts are joyful, for we have seen [our] salvation,
and now with the angels and saints
we praise you for ever [and ever].
Amen.

POSSIBLE GROUP GROUND RULES

Faith Sharing is:

Regular: I will do my best to make all sessions.

Voluntary: No one is required to share. The tone is invitational. Verbal participation is encouraged but not demanded.

Not Interrupted: When someone is sharing, everyone listens before commenting or speaking. Side conversations are avoided; one person at a time.

Not Contradicted: The sharing is based on the person's own experience, so conclusions or critiques of what is shared are not appropriate. Avoid trying to take away feelings with comments like, *You shouldn't feel that way.*

Done In "I" Language: beginning with *I think* or *I feel* rather than *Mary said* or *Joe thinks.*

Confidential: What is said in the group stays in the group.

(These ground rules are drawn from Joye Gros' *Theological Reflection,* Loyola Press, 2002. Groups are free to alter them as they wish.)

I agree with the group ground rules.   (Signature and Date)

PLANNING MY OWN FUNERAL?

* Note: Some of these parts will come easy.
Take your time with those that do not.

Week 1 - VIGIL	**3**
A Hebrew View	6
Finding God in Death?	7
In Other Words	8
* Some Thoughts On My Dying	11
* Family Tree	12
* A Testament of Life	13
* Burial Instructions	17
* Vigil for the Deceased	18
* Vigil Readings & Song	19
Week 2 - READINGS	**21**
Funeral Homily for Helen, a Reader	24
First Reading (list)	27
Responsorial Psalm (list)	28
Second Reading (list)	29
Gospel Reading (list)	31
* People in the Funeral Liturgy	33
* Funeral Songs and Readings	34
Week 3 - EUCHARIST	**37**
Symbols	41
Funeral Homily for Michael, a Father	44
Music (a list)	47
Week 4 - LEFT BEHIND	**51**
Thoughts On Grieving	57
Funeral Homily for Tommy, a Son	59
Blessing By An Elder	62
* To My Family	67

Now Thank We All Our God

Now thank we all our God
With heart and hands and voices,
Who wondrous things has done,
In whom this world rejoices;
Who from our mothers' arms
Has blessed us on our way
With countless gifts of love,
And still is ours today.

        Oh, may our bounteous God
        Through all our life be near us,
        With ever joyful hearts
        And blessed peace to cheer us;
        To keep us in God's grace
        And guide us when perplexed
        And free us from all ills
        In this world and the next.

All praise and thanks to God
Our Abba now be given,
With Son and Spirit too
Who reign in highest heaven:
The one eternal God,
Whom heaven and earth adore!
For thus it was, is now,
And shall be evermore.

Martin Rinckart, 1586-1649, Translated by Catherine Winkworth, 1829-1878, altered

1

VIGIL

Opening Prayer: Prayer From the Prefaces
(see page *iii*) all together.

Song (page 2): Now Thank We All Our God

Review together Possible Group Ground Rules.
(see page *iv*.)

Reader: A reading from the book of Wisdom:
Wisdom 3:1-6, 9

The souls of the just are in the hand of God,
And no torment shall touch them.
They seemed, in the view of the foolish, to be dead;
And their passing away was thought an affliction
And their going forth from us, utter destruction.
But they are in peace.
For if before men, indeed, they be punished,
Yet is their hope full of immortality;
Chastised a little,
They shall be greatly blessed,
Because God tried them
And found them worthy of himself.
As gold in the furnace, he proved them,
And as sacrificial offerings he took them to himself.
Those who trust in him shall understand truth,
And the faithful shall abide with him in love:
Because grace and mercy are with his holy ones,
And his care is with his elect.

Reader: The Word of the Lord.
All: **Thanks be to God.**

Then group members take turns reading the background:

An old mentor enjoyed exclaiming, *"Have you lost your mind?"* Just thinking about asking people to spend four weeks to plan their own funerals, brought this old mentor haunting me, *"Have I lost my mind?"*

Then people in the parish began telling me this craziness is the good kind. When I made arrangements for my own funeral, which I expect to happen some time in the next fifty years, surprise, I began to sense God's peaceful presence, and I began to feel a bit more alive.

Perhaps the philosophers are correct, and all our fears are rooted in our fear of dying. If this is your greatest fear, then this may be the best spiritual exercise for you to make this year. The consensus of the faith sharing groups who took this journey in the Fall of 2004 was that they laughed more than ever before.

In his *Rule* for monks, at #47 of his 72 *tools* of the spiritual craft, Saint Benedict advises

keep daily your death before you.

From studies of the initiation rituals of primitive cultures we learn that one of the five vital lessons that every culture needs each young person entering adulthood to absorb is that *you are going to die.*

Perhaps it is the very fear we have of death and burial, funerals and funeral homes, mourning and grieving, and the pain that accompanies separation, perhaps this fear is the most important reason for us to enter such a process, and *be not afraid.*

Since all of my direct ancestors have now *gone before us marked with the sign of faith,* for me to attend a funeral is for me to attend all of their funerals.

A HEBREW VIEW

Weep for the mourners, not for the departed; the departed is at peace while the mourners are left in their sorrow.

Life is a passing shadow - the shadow of a bird in flight. The bird flies away and there is neither bird nor shadow.

Do not act as though you expect to live eternally. Live as though this day were your last. Let each day be spent in repentance and good deeds.

The wicked are considered dead even during their lifetime; the righteous are considered alive even after they have died.

The righteous need no monuments; their good deeds are their memorials.

When a person enters the world, his hands are clenched as though eager to grasp everything in sight. But when he departs this world, his hands are open wide as though to indicate: "See! I take nothing with me."

The soul which God gave you was pure; return it to God in the same state.

One good deed leads to another, as every evil deed leads to more wrongdoing. Better is one hour of repentance and good deeds in this world than the whole life of the world to come. It is not in our power to explain the well-being of the wicked or the tribulations of the righteous. Just as we praise God in time of joy, we should acknowledge God in time of sorrow.

Whatever God does, God does for the best.

From "Selection from the Talmud" for a Jewish Memorial Service

FINDING GOD IN DEATH?

We overcome death by finding God in it.

In itself, death is an incurable weakness of corporeal beings, complicated in our world, by the influence of an original fall. It is the sum and type of all the forces that diminish us, and against which we must fight without being able to hope for a personal, direct and immediate victory. Now the great victory of the Creator and Redeemer in the christian vision, is to have transformed what is in itself a universal power of diminishment and extinction into an essentially life-giving factor. God must, in some way or other, make room for himself, hollowing us out and emptying us, if he is finally to penetrate into us. And in order to assimilate us in him, we must break the molecules of our being so as to recast and re-model us. The function of death is to provide the necessary entrance into our inmost selves. It will make us undergo the required dissociation. It will put us into the state organically needed if the divine fire is to descend upon us. And in that way its fatal power to decompose and dissolve will be harnessed to the most sublime operations of life. What was by nature empty and void, a return to bits and pieces, can, in any human existence, become fullness and unity in God.

From *The Divine Milieu,* Pierry Teilhard de Chardin, S.J.
Harper and Row, 1965.

IN OTHER WORDS:

Solomon said to his son, "Be not afraid."
Proverbs 3:25

Gabriel said to Mary, "Be not afraid."
Luke 1:30

The angel of the Lord said to Joseph, "Be not afraid."
Matthew 1:20

After the great catch, Jesus said to Simon,
"Be not afraid."
Luke 5:10

Concerning those who would persecute them,
Jesus said to the Twelve, "Be not afraid."
Matthew 10:26; Luke 12:4

When Jesus walked on the water toward the Twelve,
he said, "Be not afraid."
Matthew 14:27; Mark 6:50; John 6:20

At the Transfiguration, Jesus said to
Peter, James and John, "Be not afraid."
Matthew 17:7

After he had risen, Jesus said to Mary and
Mary Magdalene, "Be not afraid."
Matthew 28:10

The Lord said to Paul, "Be not afraid."
Acts 18:9

An angel of God said to Paul, "Be not afraid."
Acts 27:24

The Lord is my helper, I will not be afraid.
Hebrews 13:6

Rare is the funeral that is welcomed. They are not fun, and yet they force us to stop the treadmill of daily life and take a good look at ourselves and those we love. How often, I have noticed, is a funeral the setting that our Lord uses to wake up his son or his daughter to an awareness of his or her inheritance as a child of God. How often it is when it seems nothing else will, that a funeral gets a good person to attend to his or her humanity and vocation. Because of this, one well-known speaker on the Church's role in social justice says he would trade everything else the Church does in evangelization for good homilies at funerals (and weddings).

To pray about and plan my own funeral can be a statement to those I love that their faith matters to me.

When I was a deacon in Chicago, I met a four-year-old girl a couple of weeks after she went to Sunday mass for the first time. Her mother shared with me that after the praying, preaching, standing, kneeling, singing, silence and speaking were done, this little girl sat in that pew with her arms crossed. Mother asked daughter, "What's wrong?" and daughter accused mother, "You did not tell me that this guy Jesus was dead." The church had the big and typically Catholic crucifix hanging behind the altar. Was it the corpus, the image of the crucified Jesus that got her attention? Or was it references in the Eucharistic Prayer to his dying that got her, or something in the readings? Something in a song?

Whatever it was, the young mother realized that indeed she had not really talked about Jesus on the cross.

So she did. And then spoke of Christ risen to new life, and the promise that his rising to new life holds for us, when we die, and here today as we seek to do good, love one another, and be fully alive.

This four-year-old girl said then, "OK, but I'm gonna have to think about it." And so she did. She had heard of Jesus as the good and holy man, the Son of God, worthy of all worship, and her friend. She knew Jesus the way we experience him, as Christ in our midst, even as Christ alive in each other. She first came to know the Risen Lord, and then, in her fifth year of life, began meeting Jesus on the cross.

For most of us, growth as a disciple comes gradually, slowly, over a lifetime. As we reflect on any life, in some way it will teach us about being a disciple. None of us is perfect. As long as we are taking in the breath of life, our God is still shaping each of us into the man or woman God created us to be. Still, if in our living we have loved at all, then we have given some kind of witness to the resurrection of Jesus.

A funeral begins with a death, which is always preceded by a life: a life of one human person created in God's image, redeemed by God's Son, and helped every moment of each day by the Holy Spirit.

So, funeral planning begins with *data* about one human being, the details of one human life. We will often find God in those details. You have four weeks to work on the next eight pages.

Some Thoughts On My Dying

Name _____

Address _____

City, State _____ *Zip* _____

Date of Birth _____ *Place of Birth* _____

Date of Baptism _____ *Place* _____

Other Sacraments _____

_____

While I am dying,

☐ I very much want someone I love to be with me.

☐ I would be happy to be alone.

☐ I would enjoy someone occasionally reading from:

_____

_____

☐ I would enjoy occasionally some music (video?):

_____

_____

☐ Remember, ☐ I am (☐ *I am not*) an organ donor.
 See my ☐ driver license, or:_____

Family Tree

Spouse _____

_____

Father _____

    Place born _____   *date* _____

Mother _____

    Place born _____   *date* _____

Maternal Grandparents _____

Paternal Grandparents _____

Children, Stepchildren, Grandchildren _____

_____

_____

Brothers, Sisters, Stepbrothers, Stepsisters _____

_____

_____

Brothers-in-law, Sisters-in-law _____

_____

Other Family Members, Aunts, Uncles, Cousins, Special Friend

_____

A Testament Of Life

Of course, we all know that a human person is never just a set of facts. The Jesuit Priest, Anthony de Mello, S.J., offers a wonderful spiritual exercise, a way for us to reflect on our one particular life:

I imagine that today I am to die… I ask for time to be alone and write down for my family and friends a sort of testament for which the points that follow could serve as chapter titles:

1. *These things I have loved in life:*

    Things I tasted,

    looked at,

    smelled,

    heard,

    touched.

2. *These experiences I have cherished:*

3. *These ideas have brought me liberation:*

4. *These beliefs I have outgrown:*

5. *These convictions I have lived by:*

6. *These are the things I have lived for:*

7. *These insights I have gained in the school of life:*

   insights into God,

   the world,

   human nature,

   Jesus Christ,

love,

religion,

prayer.

8. *These risks I took, these dangers I have courted:*

9. *These sufferings have seasoned me:*

10. *These lessons life has taught me:*

11. *These influences have shaped my life (persons, occupations, books, events):*

12. *These scripture texts have lit my path:*

13. These things I regret about my life:

14. These are my life's achievements:

15. These persons are enshrined within my heart:

16. These are my unfulfilled desires:

I choose an ending for this document:

    a poem - my own or someone else's;

    or a prayer;

    a sketch or a picture from a magazine;

    a scripture text;

    *or anything that I judge would be
an apt conclusion to my testament.*

Burial Instructions

I would like for my obituary to be written, if possible, (☐ concisely)

    by: _____

I would prefer if any memorial gifts be made to:

_____

_____

I would like for this mortuary to take care of the body:

_____

I prefer to be   ☐ embalmed   ☐ buried promptly

    ☐ buried wearing _____

    ☐ buried at this cemetery: _____

    ☐ with this kind of casket: _____

    ☐ cremated, with ashes inurned at this cemetery:

    _____

    ☐ epitaph for the tombstone? _____

    ☐ prayer for the memorial card: _____

    _____

Vigil For The Deceased

The vigil is usually held the night before the Funeral Mass. It begins the entire Funeral Liturgy. It can be located at a private home or at a funeral home, and many parishes welcome hosting the vigil in the church or narthex. The vigil is most appropriately held in the presence of the body, with an open casket. The promise of the resurrection makes it possible for us to mourn together in the presence of the body. Often, this can be very helpful for friends and family who were unable to visit the deceased before his or her death, as a powerful opportunity to absorb the reality of the human death of a loved one. The Vigil is the most appropriate time for friends and family to share stories and memories about the one who has died. Our stories become part of our identity, and this helps us to give due honor to our relationships that do not end in death.

I prefer that visitation with the family be held ☐ *in the church and narthex or parish hall.* ☐ *in a funeral home.* ☐ *at home.* ☐ *wherever the family wants it to be.*

Vigil Leader _____

Vigil Reader _____

Vigil Song Leader _____

Please ask this person to be the first to tell a story at the Vigil _____

Please ask this military branch, fraternal/civic organization, or prayer group (_____) to stand honor guard at the ☐*vigil* ☐ *graveside* ☐*before the funeral.*

Vigil Readings & Song

It is always appropriate that a passage or some passages of Sacred Scripture be read at the Vigil. The Funeral Rite suggests these readings, though others may be chosen. Some people choose only one reading for the vigil.

☐ 1 John 3:1-2 ✠ *We shall see God as God is.*
☐ Psalm 103 ✢ *The Lord is kind and merciful.*
☐ Gospel: John 14:1-6 ♦ *Do not let your hearts be troubled.*
☐ or _____

The Vigil may also be a great opportunity for a favorite meaningful song which may not be suitable for the funeral Mass.

Before we had an official Rite for the Vigil for the Deceased, Catholics sensed the need for some way of praying at the wake, and so spread the devotional practice of praying the rosary on the evening before the funeral Mass. If there are two evenings of visitation, perhaps the first evening of visitation would be a good time to pray the rosary. Another possibility would be at three o'clock on the afternoon of the Vigil. And some families prefer to pray the rosary in lieu of the Vigil.

You will want to give consideration to the number of people who are familiar with praying the rosary. I have been called to lead the rosary as the only living Catholic in the room; the scripture of the Vigil would have been more helpful for the families.

☐ *I prefer that the rosary be prayed* ☐ *as part of the Vigil*
  ☐ *instead of the Vigil* ☐ *by the family at a time other than the Vigil*

Reflection

There is not enough time in one faith-sharing session for any of us to answer all of the questions offered in this first week. May we suggest simply using these pages and pages 33, 34 and 67 to begin the process. Complete first the parts that come easier to you, and use the next three weeks to reflect on the others. You may want to use a pencil, and keep handy an eraser.

1. Describe any uncomfortable feelings about planning your own funeral.

2. Do you carry in your memory a funeral that did not go well?

3. What was the most beautiful or healing funeral for you?

Closing Prayer

Are there any intercessions from the group?

Repeat the "Prayer From the Prefaces" on page iii.

Conclude with a Song, on either page 2 or page 21.

2

READINGS

Opening Prayer: Prayer From the Prefaces
(see page *iii*) all together.

Shepherd of Souls
If no one knows the melody, read the verses together.

Shepherd of souls, refresh and bless
Your chosen pilgrim flock
With manna in the wilderness,
And water from the rock.

We would not live by bread alone,
But by your Word of grace,
In strength of which we travel on
To our abiding place.

Be known to us in breaking bread,
But do not then depart;
Savior, abide with us and spread
Your table in our heart.

Text: James Montgomery, 1825, altered; Music: ST. AGNES, John B. Dykes, 1866.

Reader: A reading from the Letter of Paul to the Romans:
Romans 8:31b-35, 37-39

If God is for us, who can be against us?
He who did not spare his own Son
but handed him over for us all,
how will he not also give us
everything else along with him?
Who will bring a charge against God's chosen ones?
It is God who acquits us.
Who will condemn us?
It is Christ Jesus who died, rather, was raised,
who also is at the right hand of God,
who indeed intercedes for us.
What will separate us from the love of Christ?
Will anguish, or distress, or persecution, or famine,
    or nakedness, or peril, or the sword?
No, in all these things we conquer overwhelmingly
through him who loved us.
For I am convinced that neither death, nor life,
    nor angels, nor principalities,
    nor present things, nor future things,
    nor powers, nor height, nor depth,
    nor any other creature
will be able to separate us from the love of God in
    Christ Jesus our Lord.

Reader: The Word of the Lord.
All: **Thanks be to God.**

Then group members take turns reading the background:

The word of God gives comfort to the afflicted and afflicts the comfortable. So, which do we want at a funeral? Most would say that a funeral is for the living, to give them comfort and reassure them with hope.

The Bible, the word of God, has endured to a large degree because it has assisted humanity in dealing with and living through the unwelcome and tragic events. In the New Testament, the early Christians knew well the anxiety and tears that faith is sooner or later called upon to bear.

That Christ shed tears is recorded only twice in the gospels. One was over the death of a city, Jerusalem. The other was over the death of a friend, Lazarus. By shedding tears himself, Jesus made holy the tears we shed over the loss of a loved one. Liturgikon, 1977

Jesus understands. God knows we must cry. It is what we do when we hurt, the human thing. Yet our sorrow will somehow turn into joy in faith. God of mercy, the source of consolation, is with us, in family and friends, in God's word, and in our quiet time.

So, when planning our own funeral, it is good for us to keep in mind how people might respond to the word as it is proclaimed. Since people we love will be praying for us at our funeral, perhaps the word that will bring the most comfort is the one that is paired with the awareness that these particular words brought comfort and hope to us in the living of our faith.

Funeral Homily for Helen, a Reader

Helen was one of three parishioners who died on February 1, 2001. Helen had been told only three days earlier of the magnitude of the cancer hidden behind her big heart. On that day, expecting ten more months of living, she began to plan her funeral, choosing these readings:

Isaiah 25:6a, 7-9 ✪ *The Lord God will destroy death forever.*
Psalm 23 ❆ *Shepherd me, O God . . .*
Revelation 21:1-5a, 6b-7 ✠ *I saw a new heaven and a new earth…*
John 6:51-58 ♦ *I am the living bread . . .*

> We have a history.
> In our history, there is always something new.
> And the source of our newness, our newness of life,
>   is the love of God.

Part of Helen's history is this place of word and sacrament.
Part of Helen's newness is in our ancient ritual on this
    modern afternoon.
And Helen's very fullness of love
    is in this gathering of people.
We have been honored to hear Helen proclaim
    the word of God, reading scripture, out loud,
    with her gift of confident assurance.
And we know, do we not, that this is one of the ways Christ
is present to us: in the proclamation and hearing of the word.
As hungry to say the word as to hear it, she was usually
    the first to present herself on a holy day of obligation,
    a feasting of God, the first to make that offer:
            Do you need a reader?

No polished actor was this reader.
In her voice, the word came from a depth of humanity.
In public proclamation and in the struggles of private prayer,
Helen touched a hunger to live awash in the word of God.
Helen has also taught us some grand things
> about table fellowship. All are welcome.
>
> Feasting is to be enjoyed. And don't be bashful.

A hunger for the Eucharist is something we can see
> from a mile away.
>
> This hunger of hers could erupt into controversy,
>> as it did not long ago,
>
> when she perceived that someone was trying
>> to keep her from taking communion to the sick.
>
> The controversy subsided, but not the hunger.

The table communion of Jesus Christ means also being open
to learning new things that can be learned from others.
> And so, she kept on being a student,
> even into this new millenium, a student of Spanish,
> wondering all the while at how even a rudimentary skill
> might be used by God for good . . .

And Helen has taught us a bit about what it is to serve.
> It would not be possible to compose
>> a litany that would catch it all.
>
> One ministry she claimed affected me:
>> that of training new pastors.

But, wait a minute:
isn't this supposed to be all about Jesus Christ?
Aren't we really here to celebrate the Resurrection?
> Helen was quite clear that she wanted this to be
>> a celebration, something happy.
>
> But sometimes it is hard to dance.

So, even if we cannot yet engage fully in dance,
we will take a step by singing about dancing,
and two-step into this liturgy of gratitude.
Thus we sing of Jesus Christ,   the alpha and the omega,
>   host of the new Jerusalem,
>   the shepherd who is good,
>   the host who has prepared a banquet.
Thus we sing of God the Father,
>   who provides on the mountain,
>   who wipes away every tear,
>   who is our source of living bread,
>   who chose our midst as dwelling place.
Thus we sing, in the age of the Holy Spirit of God,
>   our ever present helper and guide.
For me, it is enough to remember what love is,
and to proclaim again those words Isaiah foretold to be said "on that day:"

> Behold our God, to whom we looked to save us!
> This is the Lord for whom we looked;
> let us rejoice and be glad . . .

First Reading

FROM THE OLD TESTAMENT

☐ 2 Maccabees 12:43-46 ✿ *He acted in an excellent and noble way as he had the resurrection of the dead in view.*

☐ Job 19:23-27a ✿ *I know that my Vindicator lives.*

☐ Wisdom 3:1-9 (or 3:1-6, 9) ✿ *The souls of the just are in the hand of God.*

☐ Wisdom 4: 7-15 ✿ *An unsullied life, the attainment of old age.*

☐ Isaiah 25: 6a, 7-9 ✿ *He will destroy death forever.*

☐ Lamentations 3:17-26 ✿ *It is good to hope in silence for the saving help of the Lord.*

☐ Daniel 12:1-3 ✿ *But the wise shall shine brightly.*

FROM THE NEW TESTAMENT (during the Easter Season)

☐ Acts of the Apostles 10:34-43 (or 10:34-36, 42-43)
✠ *In truth, I see that God shows no partiality.*

☐ Revelation 20:11—21:1 ✠ *Then I saw a new heaven and a new earth.*

* FROM THE OLD TESTAMENT, FUNERALS FOR CHILDREN

☐ * Isaiah 25:6a, 7-9 ✿ *He will destroy death forever.*

☐ * Lamentations 3:22-26 ✿ *His mercies are not spent.*

NEW TESTAMENT (during the Easter Season) CHILDREN

☐ * Revelation 7:9-10, 15-17 ✠ *God will wipe away every tear from their eyes.*

☐ * Revelation 21:1a, 3-5a ✠ *I, John, saw a new heaven and a new earth.*

Responsorial Psalm

☐ * Psalm 23 ✪ *The Lord is my shepherd; there is nothing I shall want.*

☐ * Psalm 25 ✪ *To you, O Lord, I lift my soul.*

☐ Psalm 27 ✪ *The Lord is my light and my salvation.*

☐ * Psalm 42 ✪ *My soul is thirsting for the living God: when shall I see him face to face?*

☐ Psalm 63 ✪ *My soul is thirsting for you, O Lord my God.*

☐ Psalm 103 ✪ *The Lord is kind and merciful.*

☐ Psalm 116 ✪ *I will walk in the presence of the Lord in the land of the living.*

☐ Psalm 122 ✪ *I rejoiced when I heard them say: let us go to the house of the Lord.*

☐ Psalm 130 ✪ *Out of the depths, I cry to you, Lord.*

☐ Psalm 143 ✪ *O Lord, hear my prayer.*

* RESPONSORIAL PSALMS, FUNERALS FOR CHILDREN

☐ * Psalm 148 ✪ *Let all praise the name of the Lord.*

Second Reading

FROM THE NEW TESTAMENT

☐ Romans 5:5-11 ✠ *Hope does not disappoint.*

☐ Romans 5:17-21 ✠ *Where sin increased, grace overflowed all the more.*

☐ * Romans 6:3-9 (or 6:3-4,8-9) ✠ *We too might live in newness of life.*

☐ Romans 8:14-23 ✠ *I consider that the sufferings of this present time are as nothing compared with the glory to be revealed for us.*

☐ Romans 8:31b-35, 37-39 ✠ *What will separate us from the love of Christ?*

☐ * Romans 14:7-9, 10c-12 ✠ *Whether we live or die, we are the Lord's*

☐ * 1st Corinthians 15:20-28 (or 15:20-23) ✠ *So too in Christ shall all be brought to life.*

☐ 1st Corinthians 15:51-57 ✠ *Where, O death, is your sting?*

☐ 2nd Corinthians 4:14 — 5:1 ✠ *Our inner self is being renewed day by day.*

☐ 2nd Corinthians 5:1, 6-10 ✠ *We have a building from God, eternal in heaven.*

☐ Philippians 3:20-21 ✠ *Our citizenship is in heaven.*

- ☐ * 1ˢᵗ Thessalonians 4:13-18 ✠ *Thus we shall always be with the Lord.*

- ☐ 2ⁿᵈ Timothy 2:8-13 ✠ *If we have died with him we shall also live with him.*

- ☐ 1ˢᵗ John 3:1-2 ✠ *We shall see him as he is.*

- ☐ 1ˢᵗ John 3:14-16 ✠ *the way we came to know love was that he laid down his life for us.*

* FROM THE NEW TESTAMENT, FUNERALS FOR CHILDREN, plus:

- ☐ * Ephesians 1:3-5 ✠ *He chose us in him.*

OTHER READINGS PEOPLE HAVE CHOSEN

- ☐ Ecclesiastes 3:1-15 ✿ *A time to be born, and a time to die…*

- ☐ Romans 8:24-27 ✠ *…we hope for what we do not see…*

- ☐ 1ˢᵗ Corinthians 2:6-10 ✠ *Eye has not seen, ear has not heard.*

- ☐ 1ˢᵗ Corinthians 13 ✠ *Love is patient, love is kind…*

- ☐ 2ⁿᵈ Timothy 4:6-8 ✠ *I have kept the faith…*

Gospel Reading

☐ Matthew 5:1-12a ♦ *The Beatitudes*

☐ *Matthew 11:25-30♦ *Come to me and I will give you rest.*

☐ Matthew 25:1-13 ♦ *Behold, the bridegroom! Come out to him!*

☐ Matthew 25:31-46 ♦ *Corporal works of mercy*

☐ Mark 15:33-39; 16:1-6 (or 15:33-39) ♦ *Jesus gave a loud cry and breathed his last.*

☐ Luke 7:11-17 ♦ *Young man, I tell you, arise!*

☐ Luke 12:35-40 ♦ *For at an hour you do not expect, the Son of Man will come.*

☐ Luke 23:33, 39-43 ♦ *Jesus, remember me when you come into your kingdom.*

☐ Luke 23:44-46,50,52-53; 24:1-6a (or 23:44-46,50,52-53) ♦ *Father, into your hands I commend my spirit.*

☐ Luke 24:13-35♦ *Two of the disciples were going to Emmaus.*

☐ John 5:24-29 ♦ *Whoever hears my word and believes has passed from death to life.*

☐ * John 6:37-40 ♦ *Everyone who sees the Son and believes in him may have eternal life.*

☐ * John 6:51-59 ♦ *Whoever eats this bread will live forever.*

- ☐ John 11:17-27 (or 11:21-27) ♦ *I am the resurrection and the life.*

- ☐ * John 11:32-45 ♦ *Lazarus, come out!*

- ☐ John 12:23-28 (or 12:23-26) ♦ *If it dies, it produces much fruit.*

- ☐ John 14:1-6 ♦ *In my Father's house there are many dwellings.*

- ☐ John 17:24-26 ♦ *I wish that where I am they also may be with me.*

- ☐ John 19:17-18, 25-39 ♦ *And bowing his head he handed over his Spirit.*

* GOSPEL, FUNERALS FOR BAPTIZED CHILDREN, plus:

- ☐ * Mark 10:13-16 ♦ *The Kingdom of heaven belongs to little children.*

- ☐ * John 19:25-30 ♦ *Behold your mother.*

GOSPEL, FUNERALS FOR CHILDREN WHO DIE BEFORE BAPTISM

- ☐ Matthew 11:25-30 ♦ *Come to me and I will give you rest.*

- ☐ Mark 15:33-46 ♦ *Jesus gave a loud cry and breathed his last.*

- ☐ John 19:25-30 ♦ *Behold your mother.*

People in the Funeral Liturgy

☐ If possible, I wish the funeral to be a Mass celebration.
☐ For my own reasons, I prefer a simple Liturgy of the Word.

Please involve these people if they are willing and available:
(Pallbearers, greeters, singers, readers and gift bearers do not have to be Catholic.)

Pallbearers _____

_____

Greeters _____

Song Leader _____

Singers _____

Altar Servers _____

Placing of the Pall (at least 2 people) _____

Placing of the Christian symbol (see pg. 43) _____

Reader of First Reading _____

Responsorial Psalm ☐*Cantor, or* ☐*Reader* _____

Reader of Second Reading _____

Reader of Gospel (deacon or priest) _____

Preaching Homily (deacon or priest) _____

General Intercessions Reader _____

Gift Bearers (2 or 3 people) _____
Extraordinary Ministers of Holy Communion (3 is a good number)

_____

Remarks of Remembrance (not required) _____
(It is best to limit remarks to one person at the funeral, with the rest at the Vigil.)

Funeral Songs and Readings

Entrance Song (see page 47) _____

Placing of the Pall and Christian symbol (in silence)

First Reading, Old Testament (see page 27)

_____

Responsorial Psalm (see page 28)

_____

Second Reading, New Testament (see page 29)

_____

Gospel Reading (see page 31)

_____

In the General Intercessions (the Prayers of the Faithful), please include prayers for: _____

_____

Offertory Song (see page 47) _____

Communion Song (see page 47) _____

Meditation Song? (see page 47) _____

Incensing Song (Song of Farewell)

Recessional Song (see page 47) _____

Reflection

1. The Church teaches that the Risen Christ is present to us (1) in the bread and wine that becomes the body and blood of the Risen Lord, (2) in the word of God as it is proclaimed and heard, (3) in the gathered assembly (*There am I in the midst of them,* Mathew 18:20), and (4) in the person of the priest.
   (See the *Constitution on the Sacred Liturgy* 7)

   Does the word of God more often give me comfort or afflict me with a challenge?
   Why might this be?

2. Is there a passage or image from Sacred Scripture which calls me to it in prayer or in difficult times? Why this particular composition of God's word?

3. Is there a passage of scripture which I certainly do not want to be read at my funeral?
   Why this passage?

4. How do I see the crucifixion of Jesus in thoughts of my own mortality?

Closing Prayer

Are there any intercessions from the group?
Then (Prayers from the Blessing of Readers)

Leader The word of God calls us out of darkness into the light of faith. With the confidence of God's children let us ask the Lord to hear our prayers.

1st Reader For the Church, that we may continue to respond to the word of God which is proclaimed in our midst,
We pray to the Lord.
>> All: **Lord, graciously hear us.**

2nd Reader For all who listen as the Scriptures are proclaimed, that God's word may find in them a fruitful field,
We pray to the Lord.
>> All: **Lord, graciously hear us.**

3rd Reader For those who have not heard the message of Christ, that we may be willing to bring them the good news of salvation,
We pray to the Lord.
>> All: **Lord, graciously hear us.**

4th Reader For the readers of our parish, that with deep faith and confident voice they may announce God's saving word,
We pray to the Lord.
>> All: **Lord, graciously hear us.**

Conclude with the Song on the next page.

3

EUCHARIST

Opening Prayer: Prayer From the Prefaces
(see page *iii*) all together.

All Glory, Laud, and Honor

All glory, laud, and honor,
To you, redeemer, King,
To whom the lips of children
Make sweet hosannas ring.
The King you are of Israel,
And David's royal Son,
Beloved of the Father,
Our Royal Blessed One.

The company of angels
Are praising you on high,
With human beings too all
Creation makes reply.
The Chosen of the Covenant
With psalms before you went;
So too our praise and anthems
Before you we present.

To you, before your passion,
Apostles sang your praise;
To you, now high exalted,
Our melody we raise.
Acceptable their voices;
Hear too the praise we bring
Delight in your Beloved,
Our Savior and our King.

Text by St. Theodulph of Orleans, c. 821, Translated by John M. Neal, 1854, altered
Music by Melchior Teschner, 1613

Reader: A reading from the Gospel of Mark:
Mark 15:33-39; 16:1-6

At noon darkness came over the whole land
>until three in the afternoon.

And at three o'clock Jesus cried out in a loud voice,
>*"Eloi, Eloi, lema sabachthani?"*
>which is translated,
>"My God, my God, why have you forsaken me?"

Some of the bystanders who heard it said,
>"Look, he is calling Elijah."

One of them ran, soaked a sponge with wine,
>put it on a reed,
>and gave it to him, saying,
>"Wait, let us see if Elijah comes to take him down."

Jesus gave a loud cry and breathed his last.

The veil of the sanctuary was torn in two
>from top to bottom.

When the centurion who stood facing him
>saw how he breathed his last he said,
>"Truly this man was the Son of God!"

When the Sabbath was over,
>Mary Magdalene, Mary, the mother of James,
>>and Salome
>
>bought spices so that they might go and anoint him.

Very early when the sun had risen,
>on the first day of the week, they came to the tomb.

They were saying to one another,
>"Who will roll back the stone for us
>from the entrance to the tomb?"

When they looked up,
> they saw that the stone had been rolled back;
> it was very large.
On entering the tomb they saw a young man
> sitting on the right side, clothed in a white robe,
> and they were utterly amazed.
He said to them, "Do not be amazed!
You seek Jesus of Nazareth, the crucified.
He has been raised; he is not here.
Behold the place where they laid him."

Reader: The Gospel of the Lord.
All: **Praise to you, Lord Jesus Christ.**

Then group members take turns reading the background:

After a couple of young adult years of not going to Sunday mass, I found myself being drawn again to the Sunday celebration. While most of my friends attended a wedding at which I did not feel welcome, I helped my brother Danny work on his roof. He surprised me with his news of having attended mass the Sunday previous, and how Fr. Cunningham's homily spoke to him. This news opened up a hunger in me that I had forgotten.

The next day was Sunday, and there I went, embarrassed to have forgotten so many of the basic prayers in that short time. It felt pretty awkward.

The memory of that first mass "back" is burned in; I could make a movie of it. Unable to say out loud the entire Creed, I said the parts I could and left the rest in God's hands for later. Later would come, and that is a whole 'nother story. A powerful part of that movie is my trudging up in the communion procession, making a silent request of Jesus:

> *Lord, I believe in you,*
> *But I am not sure I believe in the Eucharist.*
> *How can I understand it?*
> *Lord, help my incomplete faith.*
> *I think you want me to receive you.*
> *I put this in your hands.*
> *Just know I love you.*
> *I need your help here.*

And the Lord helped me. In the weeks to come, I found myself at home again, and began to know the presence of the Risen Lord in the experience of being in communion with his Body.

Funny though to me now, it was not until the first Sunday mass after the death of Charlie Wolf, the man my brothers and I called "hey deddy." I had been ordained but seven months, and had last seen *Hey Deddy* after the early morning mass the week before he died. In the Eucharistic Prayer, the references to the communion of saints hit in a way they had not hit before. I got it. Not only were we remembering the Lord's Supper in a way that made it and the crucifixion and the resurrection present to us, but we were also anticipating the heavenly banquet in a way in which we already participate in it. What a mystery, but a real mystery.

Symbols

With the "real presence" of the Risen Lord, at a funeral mass we also use heavy symbols to walk through the mysteries of our faith. "Symbol" is from a Greek word meaning "something thrown together," something representing something else, whether "naturally" (e.g., lion symbolizing courage) or conventionally (e.g., flag symbolizing a country). By making other things present, symbols enter our imagination, affect our feelings and influence our behavior. Rational explanations will always fall short of the potential range of meanings expressed by some symbols. Particularly when we take up religious symbols which represent ultimate, transcendent realities, we can expect these symbols to prove inexhaustible in their significance.

EASTER CANDLE and OTHER CANDLES

The Easter candle reminds the faithful of Christ's undying presence among [us,] of his victory over sin and death, and of [our] share in that victory by virtue of our initiation. It recalls the Easter Vigil, the night when the Church awaits the Lord's resurrection and when new light for the living and the dead is kindled. During the funeral liturgy and also during the vigil service, when celebrated in the church, the Easter candle may be placed beforehand near the position the coffin will occupy at the conclusion of the procession... Other candles may also be placed near the coffin during the funeral liturgy as a sign of reverence and solemnity. (Order of Christian Funerals (OCF), 35)

HOLY WATER

Blessed or holy water reminds the assembly of the saving waters of baptism. In the rite of reception of the body at the church, its use calls to mind the deceased's baptism and initiation into the community of faith... (OCF 36)

INCENSE

Incense is used during the funeral rites as a sign of honor to the body of the deceased, which through baptism became the temple of the Holy Spirit. Incense is also used as a sign of the community's prayers for the deceased rising to the throne of God and as a sign of farewell. (OCF 37)

PALL

[It is the custom to place a pall] over the coffin when it is received at the church [or at the beginning of the funeral liturgy]. A reminder of the baptismal garment of the deceased, the pall is a sign of the Christian dignity of the person. The use of the pall also signifies that all are equal in the eyes of God (see James 2:1-9). (OCF 38)

BIBLE

A Book of the Gospels or a Bible may be placed on the coffin as a sign that Christians live by the word of God and that fidelity to that word leads to eternal life. (OCF 38)

CROSS

A cross may be placed on the coffin as a reminder that the Christian is marked by the cross in baptism and through Jesus' suffering on the cross is brought to the victory of his resurrection. (OCF 38)

FLOWERS

Fresh flowers, used in moderation, can enhance the setting of the funeral rites. (OCF 38)

CHRISTIAN SYMBOLS

Only Christian symbols may rest on or be placed near the coffin during the funeral liturgy. Any other symbols, for example, national flags, or flags or insignia of associations, [are removed from the coffin at the entrance of the church. They may be kept in the narthex to be replaced after the coffin has been taken from the church.] (OCF 38)

These **Christian symbols** have been important to me:
(See the middle of page 33.)

_____

_____

These other symbols have been important to me:

_____

_____

Funeral Homily for Michael, a Father

Michael was also one of three parishioners who died on February 1, 2001. Michael was a businessman and loved to fly. His plane had crashed a week earlier, and he was the sole survivor, with burns over 85 percent of his body. Before entering anesthesia, this husband and father of five said, "Tell my family I love them." These are the readings chosen by his family:

Lamentations 3:17-36 ✿ *It is good to wait in silence…*
Psalm 23 ✽ *Shepherd me, O God …*
1ˢᵗ Corinthians 13 ✠ *Love is patient, love is kind…*
John 6:37-40 ♦ *…and I will raise them to life …*

Our Jewish brothers and sisters have a saying:
It is difficult, if not impossible, to know who is a just person, but it is easy to see when one has died.
Our model of the just person is, of course, Jesus Christ.
Certainly a close second is another woodworker,
    another builder: Joseph.
- "loving, strong & wise," as we like to say of all good fathers.
- there when you need him.
- able to enjoy life, to have a good time.
- using the God-given gifts of a mind that seeks answers,
    a will to work and participate in God's ongoing creation,
    a freedom used for family and generosity extending,
    and an awareness of humanity
        that makes compassion possible.
- able to see the image of God
    in the ordinary human encounter.

It is easy to see when a just man has died.
In an old book from about the same year Mike and I
    were born, an old book on Christian Thought,
    Martin Luther is paraphrased:
        Faith is the acceptance of the gift of God,
        the presence of the grace of God which grasps us.
    And then, Luther is quoted directly:
        "Faith is a living and restless thing.
        The right living faith can by no means be lazy."
I remember a conversation with Mike, on a Sunday,
after mass, beyond those doors in the Narthex,
during coffee and donuts.
    Mike is patiently waiting, ready to go home,
    but resigned to stay a bit,
    and kids are running around us,
    and Mike grabs one of them, and says something.
I cannot remember the exact words,
but I do remember the message he communicated,
with conviction deep and true,
that he knew how blessed he was   in that very moment.
    There was no pretense of piety in the words he used,
    but there was that sense of faith as
    "a living and restless thing."
In our ancient funeral ritual, we use many symbols, and
we let them touch our imagination as we often touch them.
    We give honor to the bodily remains of those we love,
not to suggest that they remain as any kind of dwelling place,
but as Christians for two important reasons:
It is through body to body, sense to senses, person to person,
    that we come to know and love the person,
    the whole person.

It is also because our human body receives for us
> the waters of baptism,
> when the whole person is baptized,
> body, mind, heart and soul and strength.

Our large Easter candle is lit
> at every baptismal celebration of life,
> as a sentinel to the gospel during the Easter season,
> and at every funeral,
> which always turns into another celebration of life.

We also remember Mike's baptism in the pall,
> like the baptismal alb: a white garment, ample, flowing.

And we hear the baptismal waters,
> the background music of our lives.

We often place on the casket a symbol of the Christian life.
> A photograph of Michael and Theresa
> is a picture for us of the sacrament of marriage,
> and the giving of self in family.

Notice also the proximity of Mike's remains,
> near the table of the Lord, to remind us
> that while we experience a separation from the saints,
> and we admit the pain in that separation,
> we are also in communion with them, and they us,
> still the body of Christ.

And after we celebrate that communion in a very real way
> we will use smoke and fragrant incense,
> a sign of our prayers rising to our God,
> and smoke representing how much of it all
> we simply do not understand.

We pray, with smoke in our eyes, for God's peace.

Music

These songs, are chosen by many people for funerals. Other songs suitable for worship may be used. You may wish to borrow a hymnal.

(E) Entrance Song
(O) Offertory Song
(C) Communion Song
(M) Meditation
(R) Recessional

- ☐ Amazing Grace (O, or any)
- ☐ Ave Maria (M)
- ☐ Be Not Afraid (R)
- ☐ City of God (R)
- ☐ Come Home (children)
- ☐ Come to Me (O)
- ☐ Day by Day (M, R)
- ☐ Gift of Finest Wheat (C)
- ☐ Hail Mary, Gentle Woman (M)
- ☐ Here I Am Lord (E)
- ☐ How Great Thou Art (E,R)
- ☐ I, the Lord (R, O, M)
- ☐ I Am the Bread of Life (C)
- ☐ I Have Decided (children)
- ☐ In His Time (C, M)
- ☐ Instrumental (any)
- ☐ I Know My Redeemer (R)
- ☐ I Will Choose Christ (E,R)
- ☐ In The Garden (O)
- ☐ Jesus, what a wonder (O,C,M)
- ☐ Lord of the Dance (C)
- ☐ Morning Has Broken (E)
- ☐ Oh Lord, I am not... (O)
- ☐ Old Rugged Cross (E,O)
- ☐ On Eagle's Wings (E,R)
- ☐ Panis Angelicus (O,M)
- ☐ Prayer of St. Francis(M,R)
- ☐ Seek Ye First (E)
- ☐ Shepherd Me, O God (Ps23)
- ☐ Song of the Body…(C)
- ☐ There is a Longing (E,C)
- ☐ They'll Know We(children)
- ☐ This is the Day(children)
- ☐ We Will Rise Again (R)
- ☐ What Wondrous Love(M,C,O)
- ☐ When the Saints (E,R)
- ☐ Wind Beneath…(M)
- ☐ You Are Mine (O,M)
- ☐ You Are Near (E,C)
- ☐ _____

Reflection

1. The Church teaches that the Risen Christ is present to us (1) in the bread and wine that becomes the body and blood of the Risen Lord, (2) in the word of God as it is proclaimed and heard, (3) in the gathered assembly (*There am I in the midst of them,* Mathew 18:20), and (4) in the person of the priest.

   (See the *Constitution on the Sacred Liturgy* 7)

   Does it make any difference for me to know that a particular celebration of the Eucharist is being offered for someone I know?

2. What does the "real presence" of the Eucharist mean to me? How has my understanding of Eucharist developed over the years?

3. Do I find myself at Sunday Mass more often reflecting on the past event of the Lord's Supper, the heavenly banquet, or my life in the here and now?

4. How would I feel if a co-worker, neighbor, or friend who is not Catholic asked me to conduct a graveside funeral service for his or her family member?

Closing Prayer

Adapted from a Leaflet Missal prayer prayed by Michael's Theresa

Are there any intercessions from the group? Then, a good reader:

My God, your presence is everywhere.
Your beauty concealed we sense in fragrant blooms and
 flourishing plants, and in the stately trees with their
 branches of grace.
Your splendor all speaks from the lofty, the towering
 mountains.
Your generosity sings in the fertile, the smiling valleys.
The vast seas, too, with their mighty tides and roaring waves
 proclaim you.
Thunder and lightning of the summer storm bespeak your
 majesty.
The gentler waters of brook and lake reveal your mildness
 and mercy.
Skies open to wing give us vision flying to the edge of
 sunlight, and peace.
Thus you pervade, Lord, your whole creation.

May all the marvels of your presence fill us with praise,
 thanksgiving and joy.
May we ever adore you, the maker, sustainer, and lavish
 giver of good things.
May we preserve unspoiled the glory of all you have made
 for our profit and enjoyment.
May we enhance the flowers of the field and the birds of
 the air by a prompt and ready obedience
 to your most holy will.
This crowning gift we ask in your name, O God. Amen.

Conclude with the Song on the next page.

Praise God, from Whom All Blessings Flow

Praise God, from whom all blessings flow;
Raise hands, all creatures here below;
All heaven, praise our God, the One:
Praise Father, Holy Spirit, Son.

For majesty and mighty deeds,
With blast of horn and tambourine,
With harp and dance and flute and string,
Let every human breath now sing.

Give praise to reach the mighty dome,
Give praise with cymbals, crashing sound,
Give praise with lyre and blessed skill,
Praise God to wake the holy hill.

Praise God, from whom all blessings flow;
Raise hands, all creatures here below;
All heaven, praise our God, the One:
Praise Father, Holy Spirit, Son.

Text from Psalm 150 by Thomas Ken, 1695, altered, Music OLD HUNDREDTH,
first published in *Genevan Psalter*, 1551
Verses 2 and 3 from Psalm 150 by Stephen Joseph Wolf, 2009

4

LEFT BEHIND

Opening Prayer: Prayer From the Prefaces
(see page *iii*) all together.

Song (page 50):
Praise God, from Whom All Blessings Flow

Reader: **A reading from the Gospel of Luke:**
Luke 24:13-16, 28-35

That very day, the first day of the week,
> two of the disciples of Jesus were going
> to a village called Emmaus,
> seven miles from Jerusalem,
> and they were conversing about all the things that
>> had occurred.

And it happened that while they were conversing
> and debating,
>> Jesus himself drew near and walked with them,
>> but their eyes were prevented from recognizing him.

As they approached the village to which they
> were going,
>> he gave the impression that he was going on farther.

But they urged him, "Stay with us,
> for it is nearly evening and the day is almost over."

So he went in to stay with them.
And it happened that, while he was with them at table,
> he took bread, said the blessing,
> broke it, and gave it to them.

With that their eyes were opened and they
> recognized him,
>> but he vanished from their sight.

Then they said to each other,
> "Were not our hearts burning within us
> while he spoke to us on the way and
>> opened the Scriptures to us?"

So they set out at once and returned to Jerusalem
>   where they found gathered together
>   the Eleven and those with them, who were saying,
>   "The Lord has truly been raised and has appeared
>   > to Simon!"
Then the two recounted
>   what had taken place on the way
>   and how he was made known to them in the
>   > breaking of the bread.

Reader: The Gospel of the Lord.
All: **Praise to you, Lord Jesus Christ.**

Then group members take turns reading the background:

> As the story goes, Jesus is walking around
> heaven and goes to Peter at the front gate.
> "Peter," says Jesus, "I keep seeing these folks
> who you know and I know ought not be here.
> What gives?" Peter braces himself and says:
> "Lord, I am doing my job. But they just go
> around to the back gate and your mother
> lets them in."

I love that little joke, because it captures so many of the Catholic sensibilities, including God's desire that all be saved, hell as a reminder of the great gift of freedom in which we also pray that no one is there, and simple trust in God's mercy. Perhaps indeed the shortest path to real connection with a good person is to get to know his or her mother. To finger a bead and say, "holy mother of God, pray for us sinners, now and at the hour of our death" is to place our trust in God's mercy.

When someone dies for whom we care, we sit at the center of the mystery of what it means to be a human being, a child of God, created in God's own image, an adopted child of God, a joint heir, a co-heir with Christ. The mystery is the real hope and true faith that this child of God is in a good place. We hear it in prayerful tones, words of great respect, and in wonderful jokes and wondering about what heaven is like, with people we know helping to run the show, the house with many rooms for dwelling.

The mystery is also in the pain of loss, of separation that we feel. Dietrich Bonhoeffer, who knew suffering in the last century, wrote to his niece Renate and her husband Eberhard,

> *Nothing can make up for the absence of someone whom we love,*
> *and it would be wrong to try to find a substitute;*
> *we must simply hold out and see it through.*
> *That sounds very hard at first,*
> *but at the same time it is a great consolation,*
> *for the gap, as long as it remains unfilled,*
> *preserves the bonds between us.*

It is nonsense to say that God fills the gap;
God doesn't fill it, but on the contrary, keeps it empty
and so helps us to keep alive our former communion with
  each other, even at the cost of pain.

Dietrich Bonhoeffer, Letters and Papers from Prison,
Macmillan, 1971, page 176.

A close friend from high school and college spent the last years of her young life in a nursing home. One of Heidi's friends wrote a poem, and kept it hanging on her door. It was a long poem, full of questioning and incomprehension. It was also a bold proclamation of hope, that Christ might be speaking his word to her, in her heart, to her inmost being, in beautiful ways that we could not begin to comprehend with our healthy faculties, but in a way that she might hear with clarity.

It is still a mystery to me, why the two disciples are leaving Jerusalem on Easter morning, going to Emmaus. But what else ought they do, but go home? Jesus has, after all, died. Even as they make their way back home, Jesus joins them, to be with them, to give them a surprising, a new, a totally unexpected hope, that he is still alive, Christ in their midst. And they rush back.

Those we leave behind will experience the pain of the loss of separation. This is the cost of love, and to not risk paying it would be to accept a kind of halfway partial living. Jesus came that we might have life, and have it to the full (John 10:10). So we love, that riskiest of business, and come to learn to grieve.

I am still a student of grieving. Psalm 23 has been a true aid. I like to alternate between the psalm as it is given to us and what I call a "Lord's Prayer" version of it, alternating between praying for myself and for myself in communion with the other, whether the separation is by death or geography:

The Lord is my (our) shepherd;
  there is nothing I (we) lack.
In green pastures you let me (us) graze;
  to safe waters you lead me (us);
  You restore my (our) strength.
You guide me (us) along the right path
  for the sake of your name.
Even though I (we) walk through a dark valley,
  I (we) fear no harm for you are at my (our) side;
  your rod and staff give me (us) courage.
You set a table before me (us)
  as my (our) enemies watch;
You anoint my (our) head with oil;
  my (our) cup overflows.
Only goodness and love will pursue me (us)
  all the days of my (our) life;
I (we) will dwell in the house of the Lord
  for years to come.

When I was grieving the loss of my mother Jeanette, eight years after her death, I felt like a human failure, unable to do this grieving thing the "correct" way. I have learned that people grieve differently. It matters less how we grieve than that we do so. So, here are, without any pressure to grieve "correctly," twelve "guides" that I have found helpful. It is a message of hope.

Thoughts On Grieving

1. Not all loss is of the same magnitude or kind.

2. All loss can be the groundwork for new life.

3. Losses are unique to each individual, because we grieve more over the loss of what something meant to us than over the lost object itself.

4. Change always brings loss, even when the change is welcome.

5. As our losses are unique, so are our ways of coping with them.

6. Loss evokes a wide array of emotions, whether we admit them or not.

7. We will find the makings of our self in our own history of loss, especially in the ways we have chosen to deal with them.

8. While we cannot control the losses we experience in life, we can choose what we do with them.

9. Suffering is a mystery. The Son of God endured suffering and death out of love for and solidarity with us, but he never explained why we suffer.

10. God's grace gives us the choice of transforming loss into abundant life.

11. The Spirit dwells within us, suffers with us, consoles us, and will guide us to resurrection.

12. Growthful grieving involves three movements:
    (a) openly acknowledging what has been lost,
    (b) expressing our feelings as we acknowledge the loss,
    (c) choosing to change the things that keep us tied to the loss.

Lynn Levo, CSJ, PhD., Saint Luke Institute

Sometimes, the healing job takes some word of God. Here's some to try, in health and in healing:

◆ ◆ ◆ ◆ ◆ ◆ ◆ ◆ ◆ ◆ ◆ ◆ ◆ ◆

Sunday Morning	Psalm 100; Mark 16:5-6
Evening	Psalm 23; 1st Corinthians 15:3-8
Monday Morning	Psalm 42:1-6a; Matthew 8:1-3
Evening	Psalm 121; Ezekiel 36:24-28
Tuesday Morning	Psalm 139:1-10; Mark 3:1-5
Evening	Psalm 84:1-9; Ephesians 2:19-22
Wednesday Morning	Psalm 63:1-8; Romans 8:22-27
Evening	Psalm 131; Philippians 2:5-11
Thursday Morning	Psalm 86:1-7,11; Romans 8:14-17
Evening	Psalm 126; Luke 6:17-19
Friday Morning	Psalm 51:10-19; Luke 17:20-21
Evening	Psalm 65:4,9-13; John 14:1-7
Saturday Morning	Psalm 46; Ephesians 3:16-22
Evening	Psalm 147:1-11; Matthew 8:23-27

◆ ◆ ◆ ◆ ◆ ◆ ◆ ◆ ◆ ◆ ◆ ◆ ◆ ◆

Funeral Homily for Tommy, a Son

Tommy died in the summer before the sixth grade, of a cancer he carried since age seven.

Lamentations 3:22-26 ✿ *The mercies of the Lord are not spent.*
Psalm 42 ✼ *As a deer longs for flowing steams...*
Romans 14:7-9 ✠ *Whether we live or die, we are the Lord's.*
John 20:24-31 ♦ *"My Lord and my God."*

>How often it is that an old person who is dying
>becomes like a child.

>And how often it is that a young person who is dying
>takes on the goodness of years.

Is it possible that Tommy is only eleven years old?
It's possible, since over a quarter of that time
>he spent with cancer.

His former pastor has spoken to me of meeting with seven year old Tommy to talk about what dying is like.
>They read together a short book.
>It left a profound impact on the pastor.

The pastor at his school and I have shared our miserable efforts to check in with Tommy about his illness.
Tommy gave a clear message:
>"If you want to talk to me about something having to do with my being a fifth grade boy, then fine, let's talk.
>Otherwise, I have other things to do."

One day, while I was on the phone with his mother,
>she reported that the hospice people
>had just been to the house,
>and that they knew he was dying, but that as we spoke,
>Tommy was on a trampoline.

It was no surprise to me that Tommy would have told his
grandfather that his grandfather's breakfast club,
well to put it politely, did not meet his needs.
> That's the kind of honesty
> that one mature man uses with another.
> You can see it in his eyes,
> even in so many of those great pictures:
> a child of God who has grown comfortable
> with who he is.

Sometimes we come to a sense of who a person is by
comparison to another. I told a father of a recent high school
graduate in the parish that I wanted to speak to his son,
but couldn't catch him.
> The father referred to his son as a kind of "vapor."

Since then I have often thought of Tommy's approach to life
as a vapor moving, as a sign of something that has moved on,
but which has left a presence.
>> Like a deer that longs for running streams,
>> a deer on a trampoline.

Tommy has been a real presence to us, a full presence,
body-mind-soul. But he had an urge to get on to
>> something else, a looking to the next thing,
>> that struck me as a basic love of living,
>> and a love of being loved.

> The difficulty is that no one grows
> that comfortable with himself
> without enduring some measure of suffering.
> The word we use for that is "the cross."

Yet, we are able to actually celebrate today,
celebrate even the cross,
to say, with Tommy and with that other St. Thomas:
>> "My Lord and my God,"

because Jesus Christ has been (and is) present to us
and keeps on giving us life in his name.
A couple of weeks ago,
I dropped in on Tommy to bring him communion,
and I was greeted by an honest hunger for the eucharist,
the presence.   He was not using oxygen yet,
and it was difficult for him to find
a position in which he could breathe comfortably.
Despite my protest that he stay as he was,
he insisted on raising himself up,
uncomfortably on the lower bunk, leaning over,
with his head against the top bunk, to receive the presence
of his Lord and his God.
I have seen the same kind of reaction
with Baptists and Methodists who in their illness
are invited to listen to some word from the Bible.
Christ is present to us in so many ways:
at the celebration of the Eucharist:
in the body and blood of the risen Lord,
in the proclamation and hearing of the word,
in the gathered assembly,
"where two or more are gathered in [the] name…"
and in the priest.
Christ is also present in the poor person,
the suffering person, and in the grieving person in our midst.
In our shared grief,
we are all in the presence of our Risen Lord.
We join Thomas and Tommy, and say:
My Lord and My God! Alleluia!

Blessing by an Elder

Lord, my heart is not proud;
nor are my eyes haughty.
I do not busy myself with great matters,
with things too sublime for me.
Rather, I have stilled my soul,
hushed it like a weaned child,
Like a weaned child on its mother's lap,
so is my soul within me.
Israel, hope in the Lord, now and forever.

Praying Psalm 131 makes me laugh, because I am so often proud, haughty and such. It is also a reminder to me that God uses our parents, even in their imperfect humanity, to say something (*not everything, but something*) about who God is. Divine parenting sets us free with a blessing, just as the Abba said to Jesus in the Jordan, "**You are my beloved Son; with you I am well pleased.**" Mark1:11b Ronald Rolheiser does a great "Margaret Mead" with this touching description from nature:

Among many mammals, the mother deconstricts the baby after it is born by licking its entire body, thus stripping off the membranes which in the womb had helped cradle, protect, and feed that new life but which now bind and paralyze it. In doing this, the mother opens the newborn to life, sets it free to walk on its own, to romp in the sun. In the mammal world, this is primary blessing - the mother setting her young free, the elder giving the young their birthright. Ronald Rohlheiser, *Against An Infinite Horizon*, 2001, pg. 44

Fr. Clete Kiley has observed that it is very difficult for a man sensing a call to the priesthood to say "yes" if his father does not communicate to him somehow that this is good work for a man to do. Think of the implications this holds for every person's vocation.

As anyone who has done very much prison ministry can share, one root of much hurt in our world is a void, something missing: having been blessed by an *elder* (father, mother, grandparent, teacher, coach, mentor, priest, doctor or nurse, godparent). Of course, this is not always the case; many inmates admit that they simply made bad choices, and that none of it is anyone's fault but their own. When we are told that Jesus came to set prisoners free, he was not talking only about buildings with walls, bars, locks and guards. There are many kinds of prisons and every human being needs to be set free.

> *The heart is set free by blessing from our "elders..." It is made whole when somebody who is our "elder" affirms us, somebody who is our "elder" because something about them - they gave us birth, their superior age, or wisdom, or virtue, or talent, or position - puts them into a position where we need them to set us free, where we are dependent upon them in such a way that their affirmation or curse either binds or looses us.* (pg.44) *...To bless someone deeply is to die for that person in some real way, to really die, to give up some real life for that person... Do you want to bless a young person? Give her your job! Give him some of your power. Step back and let her assume some of the leadership you have been exercising. Let his opinion overrule yours.* (Rolheiser, pg. 40)

Why bring this up now? Just in case there is someone whom you have not yet blessed, whom you have not given the blessing out of which Jacob cheated Esau, for which they both deeply longed, over which they fought a long war. I bring this up and simply ask, is there anyone to whom you know you still need to say, "I am proud of you," "you are a good woman," "you do good work," etc.? It is better to do this in person, even with a laying on of hands, a hug, or a kiss. If for some reason this is inappropriate, you can also send a blessing in prayer.

The Church gives in her *Book of Blessings* a blessing of a son or daughter that is meant to be used by only a parent, a ritual that it would be inappropriate for even the pope to use with your son or daughter, but most appropriate for an ***elder*** of a boy, girl, man or woman:

<small>As circumstances suggest, a parent may trace the sign of the cross on the child's forehead; then saying a prayer of blessing in these or similar words (feeling free to alter it):</small>

Father,
inexhaustible source of life and author of all good,
we bless you and we thank you
for brightening our communion of love
by your gift of children.
Grant that our child will find in the life of this family
such inspiration that he/she will strive always
for what is right and good and one day, by your grace,
reach his/her home in heaven.
We ask this through Christ our Lord.
<small>Signing themselves with the sign of the cross, the parent says:</small>
May the Lord Jesus, who loved children,
Bless us and keep us in his love, now and forever. Amen.

Reflection

1. It has been suggested by some that if you wish to know the priorities of a person, take a look at his or her appointment book, checkbook, closet, and will. Would mine reflect the person I consider myself to be?

2. What experience of grieving has been more difficult or more helpful to me?

3. Am I aware of any unfinished business in my life?
   Any unfinished forgiveness?
   Any unfinished storytelling?

4. Do I need to ask forgiveness or say "I love you" to anyone?

Closing Prayer

Are there any intercessions from the group?
Then (a litany from the Funeral Rite):

Leader   Let us turn to Christ Jesus with confidence and faith in the power of his cross and resurrection.

1st Reader   Risen Lord, pattern of our life for ever:
Lord, have mercy.   All: **Lord, have mercy.**

2nd Reader   Promise and image of what we shall be:
Lord, have mercy.   All: **Lord, have mercy.**

3rd Reader   Son of God who came to destroy sin and death:
Lord, have mercy.   All: **Lord, have mercy.**

4th Reader   Word of God who delivered us from the fear of death:
Lord, have mercy.   All: **Lord, have mercy.**

5th Reader   Crucified Lord, forsaken in death, raised in glory:
Lord, have mercy.   All: **Lord, have mercy.**

6th Reader   Lord Jesus, gentle Shepherd who bring rest to our souls, giver of peace:
Lord, have mercy.   All: **Lord, have mercy.**

7th Reader   Lord Jesus, you bless those who mourn and are in pain:
Lord, have mercy.   All: **Lord, have mercy.**

Leader   May the peace of God, which is beyond all understanding, keep our hearts and minds in the knowledge and love of God and of his Son, our Lord Jesus Christ.   All: **Our Father ...**

Conclude with the Song on page 50.

To My Family

- ☐ If the parish can provide a meal in the parish hall for the family after the funeral, I would be most appreciative.

- ☐ Ask a neighbor _____ to keep an eye on the house during the funeral.

- ☐ You will want to get ten or so original copies of the death certificate. You'll need most of them.

- ☐ I encourage you to participate in the parish bereavement group. Everyone grieves in his or her own way and on his or her own timetable. Someone may be able to help you, and you may be able to help someone else.

- ☐ I ask you to remember me especially on this year's All Soul's Day (November 2).

- ☐ _____
  _____
  _____

- ☐ If you change my suggestions, I may haunt you.

- ☐ Change anything you want.

- ☐ I love you!

_____   _____
Signature   Date

www.ingramcontent.com/pod-product-compliance
Lightning Source LLC
Chambersburg PA
CBHW032017290426
44109CB00013B/690